discover more
Marine Wildlife

Sea Plants and Algae

Kaitlyn Salvatore

Published in 2025 by Britannica Educational Publishing (a trademark of Encyclopædia Britannica, Inc.) in association with The Rosen Publishing Group, Inc.
2544 Clinton Street, Buffalo, NY 14224

Copyright © 2025 by Encyclopædia Britannica, Inc. Britannica, Encyclopædia Britannica, and the Thistle logo are registered trademarks Encyclopædia Britannica, Inc. All rights reserved.

Rosen Publishing materials copyright © 2025 The Rosen Publishing Group, Inc. All rights reserved.

Distributed exclusively by Rosen Publishing.
To see additional Britannica Educational Publishing titles, go to rosenpublishing.com.

All rights reserved. No part of this book may be reproduced in any form without permission in writing from the publisher, except by a reviewer.

Editor: Brianna Propis
Book Design: Michael Flynn

Photo Credits: Cover Pinosub/Shutterstock.com; (series background) Dai Yim/Shutterstock.com; p. 4 Ton110520/Shutterstock.com; p. 5 Cheng Wei/Shutterstock.com; p. 6 Romolo Tavani/Shutterstock.com; p. 7 Dan Su Sa/Shutterstock.com; p. 8 Mike Workman/Shutterstock.com; p. 9 Ruslan Suseynov/Shutterstock.com; p. 10 Joan Carles Juarez/Shutterstock.com; p. 11 Ekky Ilham/Shutterstock.com; p. 12 yuuno0606/Shutterstock.com; p. 13 VectorMine/Shutterstock.com; p. 15 (top) Ethan Daniels/Shutterstock.com; p. 15 (bottom) Pasotteo/Shutterstock.com; p. 17 Damsea/Shutterstock.com; p. 18 Oleg Kovtun Hydrobio/Shutterstock.com; p. 19 Stock for you/Shutterstock.com; p. 20 mivod/Shutterstock.com; p. 21 TanyaPhOtOgraf/Shutterstock.com; p. 22 Kuttelvaserova Stuchelova/Shutterstock.com; p. 23 Damsea/Shutterstock.com; p. 24 Marius Dobilas/Shutterstock.com; p. 25 Andriy Nekrasov/Shutterstock.com; p. 26 J.J. Gouin/Shutterstock.com; p. 27 Vershinin89/Shutterstock.com; p. 28 Holiday.Photo.Top/Shutterstock.com; p. 29 Koldunov Alexey/Shutterstock.com.

Library of Congress Cataloging-in-Publication Data

Names: Salvatore, Kaitlyn author http://id.loc.gov/vocabulary/relators/aut
   http://id.loc.gov/authorities/names/no2024070524
   http://id.loc.gov/rwo/agents/no2024070524
Title: Sea plants and algae / Kaitlyn Salvatore.
Description: Buffalo : Britannica Educational Publishing, an imprint of
   Rosen Publishing, 2025. | Series: Discover more: marine wildlife |
   Includes index. | Audience term: Juvenile
Identifiers: LCCN 2024037638 | ISBN 9781641903660 library binding | ISBN
   9781641903653 paperback | ISBN 9781641903677 ebook
Classification: LCC QK102 S25 2025 | DDC 581.7/6--dc23/eng/20240827
LC record available at https://lccn.loc.gov/2024037638

Manufactured in the United States of America

Some of the images in this book illustrate individuals who are models. The depictions do not imply actual situations or events.

CPSIA Compliance Information: Batch #CWBRIT25. For further information contact Rosen Publishing at 1-800-237-9932.

Contents

Underwater Plants and Protists 4

Making Their Own Food 6

Plankton and Phytoplankton 10

Producers and Consumers 12

Colorful Algae 14

This Algae Is Red 16

This Algae Is Brown 18

This Algae Is Green 20

Groups of Algae 22

Mangroves and Seagrass 24

Global Warming 26

Human Use 28

Glossary 30

For More Information .31

Index 32

Underwater Plants and Protists

Plants can be found almost everywhere on Earth, including in water. Plants sustain, or support, all life on Earth. They are sources of food for people and animals, and they also make oxygen that other living things need to breathe. Hydrophytes are plants that live in the water. Some hydrophytes live completely **submerged**, while others live partially in water. All hydrophytes have traits in common, so scientists believe these plants originally came from land. But they have adapted, or changed, to live in and underwater.

Hydrilla, also known as water thyme, is a plant that lives almost completely submerged in water. Its stems can grow 20 to 30 feet (6.1 to 9.1 m) long!

Algae floats on the surface of water in this pond.

Other organisms called algae live in water too. Algae are very important because they create a large portion of Earth's oxygen, which is needed for humans and animals to breathe. Some algae look like plants, such as seaweed. However, algae are not plants or animals. Rather, they are members of a group of living things called protists.

WORD WISE
TO BE SUBMERGED MEANS TO BE COMPLETELY UNDER THE WATER'S SURFACE.

Making Their Own Food

Using a process called photosynthesis, green plants make their own food. Photosynthesis requires sunlight, water, a gas called carbon dioxide, and a substance in plants called chlorophyll. Photosynthesis is important in part because it produces oxygen. Humans and other animals need to breathe oxygen to survive. Some living things other than plants also make their food through photosynthesis. Early forms of bacteria and algae used the process of photosynthesis and still do today.

Photosynthesis is fueled by sunlight.

The process of photosynthesis requires water, sunlight, and carbon dioxide to create sugars that feed a plant.

Consider This
If photosynthesis didn't release oxygen into the atmosphere, could life on Earth still exist? Why or why not?

Photosynthesis begins when chlorophyll in plants absorbs energy from sunlight. The light energy is used to change water and carbon dioxide into oxygen and nutrients called sugars. The plants use some of the sugars to grow and store the rest. The oxygen is released back into the air or water.

There are some differences between how photosynthesis occurs above water and how it occurs underwater. Instead of getting carbon dioxide from the air that we breathe, as land plants do, both algae and marine plants (plants that live in salt water) pull carbon dioxide directly from their water environment.

Water lilies float on the surface to absorb the sunlight they need to grow and survive.

Plants are exposed to the same sunlight we are. However, plants that are submerged have a harder time getting the light they need for photosynthesis. The amount of light that penetrates, or goes through, water depends on water color, water depth, and how **turbid** the water is. This is why some marine plants have long stems with large leaves that float closer to the surface of the water—more light can be absorbed there.

WORD WISE
TURBID WATER IS CLOUDY OR MUDDY BECAUSE OF FLOATING DIRT AND OTHER SUBSTANCES IN THE WATER.

Plankton and Phytoplankton

Innumerable tiny living things float and drift in Earth's oceans. These organisms are known as plankton. They include plants, animals, and other kinds of organisms. Plankton that are animals or animal-like organisms are called zooplankton. Plankton that are plants or plant-like organisms are called phytoplankton.

Zooplankton are usually too small to see without a microscope.

Phytoplankton float in the water and create energy through photosynthesis.

These organisms are often no larger than a single cell. For example, a single-celled type of algae called a diatom is a common form of phytoplankton. Phytoplankton float near the surface of the water. Like other plants, phytoplankton undergo photosynthesis, using sunlight to produce energy. Bacteria and fungi also float in the world's waters. These can also be considered plankton.

Consider This

Since most phytoplankton get their energy from sunlight, during which seasons do you think larger amounts of phytoplankton are found in Earth's waters?

Producers and Consumers

A food chain describes the order in which living things depend on other living things for food. Every ecosystem has one or more food chains. Most food chains start with organisms that make their own food, such as plants. Scientists call them producers. Organisms that eat other living things are called consumers. Because most living things eat more than one type of animal or plant, their food chains overlap and connect, creating a food web.

Phytoplankton have an important place in the food chain that supports marine, or sea, animals and the humans who eat them. In addition to contributing to the production of oxygen, phytoplankton are also the primary food source—both directly and indirectly—of nearly all sea organisms.

Phytoplankton and algae form the base of aquatic food webs. They are eaten by primary consumers such as zooplankton, small fish, and crustaceans.

Aquatic Food Web

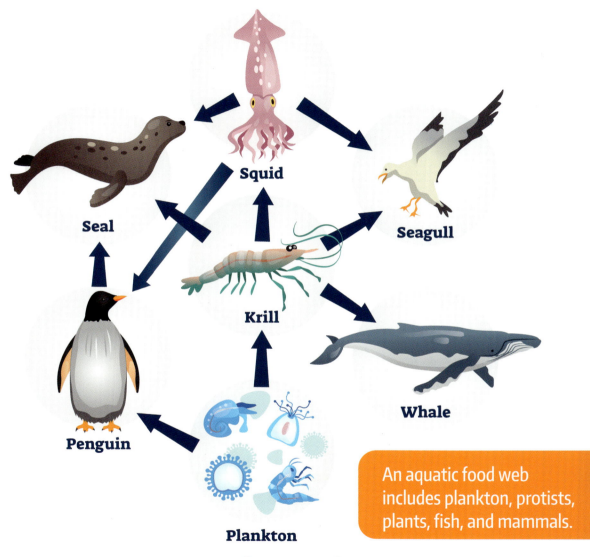

An aquatic food web includes plankton, protists, plants, fish, and mammals.

Consider This
A seal may not directly eat plankton, but plankton can still be a food source for it. How could this be?

Colorful Algae

The group called algae includes a wide variety of organisms. In general, algae are organisms made up of one or more cells containing chlorophyll. Algae differ from plants in several ways. They do not have stems or leaves, and their roots are different from plant roots. Algae also do not produce flowers or seeds as plants do. Like plants, however, most algae make their own food through photosynthesis.

There are about 27,000 different species, or types, of algae. Many types of algae consist of single cells. Other types can form colonies. Algae can be many colors, including red, brown, or green. No matter what their external color, most contain some of the green pigment chlorophyll. The size of algae varies greatly.

Certain kinds of algae, such as giant kelp, can grow to be more than 200 feet (61 m) in length.

compare and contrast

How are algae and sea plants similar? How are they different?

Chloroplasts are the parts of plants and algae cells where photosynthesis takes place.

15

This Algae Is Red

About 6,500 species of red algae can be found in marine areas. Most red algae live in tropical marine habitats, or warm parts of oceans. Most species are multicellular, meaning they have more than one cell. Red algae go through several stages of development to complete their life cycle. The red pigment in red algae allows them to absorb sunlight deep beneath the water's surface.

Several species of red algae are harvested for food. These include laver, dulse, and Irish moss. Laver is a dried, thin sheet of seaweed popular in Japanese **cuisine**. Irish moss is used in puddings, toothpaste, and ice cream. Some species of red algae are part of the formation of coral reefs and islands.

WORD WISE

CUISINE IS A STYLE OF COOKING USED BY A PARTICULAR COUNTRY, REGION, OR CULTURE. MANY TRADITIONAL JAPANESE DISHES USE ANIMALS AND PLANTS FROM THE SEA BECAUSE JAPAN IS AN ISLAND NATION.

Red algae are involved in producing about 40 to 60 percent of the oxygen used by marine ecosystems.

17

This Algae Is Brown

Brown algae is typically found along coasts and in the sea. Some can cling to rocks at the bottom of the water using structures called holdfasts. They have stalks (much like plant stems) and wide blades that are similar to leaves. These blades have small pockets of air called bladders, which aid in lifting them toward the water's surface.

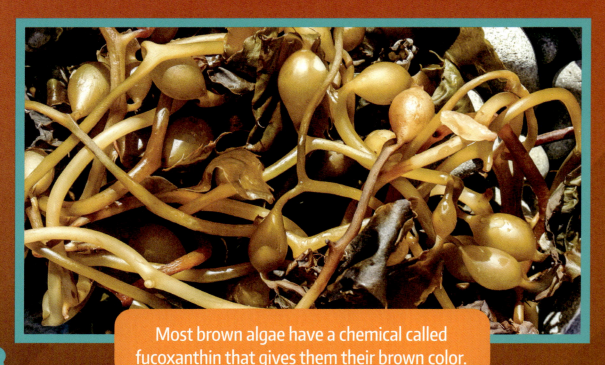

Most brown algae have a chemical called fucoxanthin that gives them their brown color.

Marine animals such as fish and sea turtles use *Sargassum* for feeding, shelter, and breeding.

A large free-floating mass of brown algae lies in an area of the western Atlantic Ocean, known as the Sargasso Sea. This algae, called *Sargassum*, is used by eels, turtles, marlins, sharks, and dolphinfish as a spawning site, or a place to reproduce. Brown algae are an important source of a gel called algin, which is used in the baking and ice cream industries to stabilize, or improve the texture of, products.

Consider This

To function, an ecosystem must be balanced—meaning each living thing in the ecosystem plays a special role so every member can survive. How does brown algae help keep its ecosystem balanced?

This Algae Is Green

Most green algae is found in fresh water. Only about 10 percent of green algae are marine. In the marine environment, some are free floating, but most live on shore rocks. Some species, such as sea lettuce, are eaten by humans. Several species live on land. Some green algae form branched threads that look like thin wires, hollow balls of cells, or broad, flat sheets.

Cyanobacteria are the most common cause of harmful algae blooms in freshwater lakes and rivers.

Chlorella is a type of green algae. Many people eat or drink forms of *Chlorella* because they're a good source of protein, vitamins, and minerals.

    Green algae are a vital link in the food chain. They are also an important source of oxygen. Nevertheless, they can also be the source of problems. Under certain conditions, many types of green algae undergo rapid and uncontrolled growth. When this happens, a "bloom" covers the water surface, blocking light from reaching the depths. This can harm other sea plants and animals.

Consider This
What sea plants and animals would be most impacted by a loss of sunlight from the rapid green algae blooms?

Groups of Algae

The large groups of red, brown, and green algae found in the oceans are also known as seaweeds. In northern areas, seaweeds form an almost continuous film over the rocks. In colder Arctic and Antarctic waters, they extend to great depths.

In the warm tropics, seaweeds are found on the floors of lagoons, and they often are associated with coral reefs and island atolls. Seaweeds can be bad for coral because they produce harmful chemicals and block the sunlight. However, recent studies have shown that seaweed also can protect coral from harmful sea stars.

The seaweeds you see washed up on beaches and other shorelines are actually algae!

There are over 12,000 species of seaweeds.

Some species of seaweeds are made up of **molecules** that can thicken almost any liquid. Over 110,230 tons (100,000 mt) of these molecules are removed from seaweed each year for various uses. Seaweed's ability to filter and clean water makes it a helpful tool when separating toxins from wastewater.

WORD WISE
MOLECULES ARE THE SMALLEST PARTICLES OF A SUBSTANCE THAT HAVE ALL ITS PHYSICAL AND CHEMICAL PROPERTIES.

Mangroves and Seagrass

Trees or bushes that grow along seashores are known as mangroves. They often have a thick tangle of roots that stick up through the mud. These roots help keep waves from washing away the dirt and sand of the coastline. The trees can grow in salty water because they are able to filter out the salt.

There are over 500,000 acres (202,343 ha) of mangroves in the coastal areas of Central and South Florida.

Sea turtles eat seagrass as a major part of their diet.

Seagrasses have roots and leaves and produce flowers and seeds. They provide valuable habitats to many invertebrates like clams, crabs, and oysters as well as many fish species. Seagrass beds are the feeding grounds of thousands of different animal species around the world. Sea turtles, manatees, and geese are a few of the animals that eat seagrass. Seagrasses can also be called paddle grass, turtle grass, and manatee grass.

Consider This

Chemicals released into the water by humans can damage or kill seagrass. What would happen to the sea turtle population if seagrass died out due to the actions of humans?

Global Warming

Earth's average surface temperature is slowly increasing every year. This trend is known as global warming. Warm temperatures are causing the polar ice to melt and ocean waters to rise, changing our shorelines. Increasing water temperature may also cause the growth of harmful algal blooms (HABs). HABs are colonies of algae that grow out of control. These may cause harm to the health of marine life because HABs produce toxins. In turn, humans can also be affected by eating fish or other organisms that contain the toxins.

Global warming is also affecting rainfall patterns, increasing both the intensity of rainfall and how long droughts last. Increased rainfall causes more runoff to enter bodies of water, which causes HABs to continue growing.

People can get sick from eating seafood contaminated with HAB-related toxins.

Another effect of HABs is that they may block the amount of light entering the water. This means less photosynthesis occurs and less oxygen enters the oceans. When less oxygen enters the ocean, fish will die.

Consider This

Pollution is a major cause of global warming. What can you do to limit the amount of pollution you produce? Think about transportation and recycling.

Human Use

Sea plants and algae have unique uses for human beings. Many people visit spas to feel healthy and revitalized, and different kinds of sea plants and algae are used at spas for health and nutritional purposes. Some spas use algae therapy to help relax and revitalize their clients. Algae or seaweed is wrapped around a person to soothe their skin and improve the flow of their blood. Red algae is also a popular food for vegetarians, or people who don't eat meat. Like meat, red algae has a lot of protein and vitamin B12.

Laver seaweed is often used in sushi. It changes color from black to green when cooked!

Studies have found that fucoidan, a carbohydrate found in brown seaweed, has anti-cancer properties.

Other types of algae can also be part of a person's diet. Ulva, or sea lettuce, is a kind of green algae that can often be found in soups and salads. Sea lettuce has lots of iodine and vitamins A, B, and C. Brown seaweeds are used to make jams, whipped cream, pie fillings, gravy, and popsicles. Your medicine or makeup products might even have traces of algae in them as well!

Consider This

The process of harvesting plants and organisms from the ocean for food is called aquaculture. How might this process be different from farming on land? Do you think one is more difficult than the other?

Glossary

absorb To take in or swallow up.

aquatic Growing or living in or often found in water.

blade The broad, flat part of a leaf.

chlorophyll The green coloring matter of plants that is necessary for photosynthesis.

colony A population of plants or animals in a particular place that belong to one species.

contaminate To make something impure by adding a poison or pollutant.

ecosystem A system made up of an ecological community of living things interacting with their environment especially under natural conditions.

extend To stretch out or reach across a distance.

fungus Living things (like molds and mushrooms) that don't have chlorophyll, live on dead or decaying matter, and were formerly considered plants.

habitat The place or type of place where a plant or animal naturally or normally lives or grows.

harvest To be gathered in a crop.

hydrophyte A plant growing in water or in waterlogged soil.

mass A large amount or number of something.

nutrient Things a plant or animal needs in order to live and grow.

organism A living thing.

protist An organism that resembles plants or animals or both, is one-celled, and that typically includes most algae.

toxin A substance produced by a living organism that is very poisonous to other organisms.

tropical Relating to warm areas of Earth near the equator.

For More Information

Books

Markovics, Joyce L. *Plankton*. Ann Arbor, MI: Cherry Lake Press, 2022.

Markovics, Joyce L. *Seaweed*. North Mankato, MN: Norwood House Press, 2023.

McCoy, Erin L. *Global Warming*. Buffalo, NY: Cavendish Square, 2019.

Websites

Britannica Kids: Algae
kids.britannica.com/kids/article/algae/
Read more about the different types of algae.

Harmful Algal Blooms and Your Health
www.cdc.gov/harmful-algal-blooms/about/index.html
Learn more about HABs and how you can prevent exposure to them.

Next Generation Science: All About Protists
www.youtube.com/watch?v=7AMr1l-ogHk
Watch this interesting video to review the group of organisms called protists.

Publisher's note to educators and parents: Our editors have carefully reviewed these websites to ensure that they are suitable for students. Many websites change frequently, however, and we cannot guarantee that a site's future contents will continue to meet our high standards of quality and educational value. Be advised that students should be closely supervised whenever they access the internet.

Index

A

algae blooms, 20, 21, 26, 27

B

bacteria, 6, 11
brown algae, 14, 18, 19, 22, 29

C

carbon dioxide, 6, 7, 8
Chlorella, 21
chlorophyll, 6, 8, 14
coral reefs, 16, 22

D

diatom, 10, 11

F

flowers, 14, 25
food chains and webs, 12, 13, 21

G

global warming, 26, 27
green algae, 14, 20, 21, 22, 29

H

holdfasts, 18

L

leaves, 9, 14, 18, 25

M

mangroves, 24

O

oxygen, 4, 5, 6, 7, 8, 12, 17, 21, 27

P

photosynthesis, 6, 7, 8, 9, 11, 14, 15, 27
phytoplankton, 10, 11, 12

R

red algae, 14, 16, 17, 22, 28
roots, 14, 24, 25

S

seagrass, 24, 25
seaweed, 5, 22, 23
seeds, 14, 25
stems, 4, 9, 14, 18
sunlight, 6, 7, 8, 9, 11, 16, 21, 22, 27

Z

zooplankton, 10, 12